Sensitivity Training

A Biblical Evaluation

Sensitivity Training

A Biblical Evaluation

Reverend G. Hette Abma

Title: *Sensitivity Training*
Subtitle: *A Biblical Evaluation*
Original Dutch title: *Sensitivitytraining*
Author: Reverend G. Hette Abma
First Dutch printing: 1981
© 2015 Maatkamp Publishing, Zelhem, Netherlands
Translation: Stephen Teeuwen (www.stephenteeuwen.nl)
Editor: Hannie Tijman (www.tijmanvertalingen.nl)
Cover design: HAS, Ede, Netherlands
ISBN-13: 978 94 91706 32 5

Website publisher: www.uitgeverijmaatkamp.nl

Table of Contents

Foreword

---

[1] Added by the publisher.

Foreword

If you think sensitivity training is some craze that passed into oblivion back in the 1970s, you're wrong. Sensitivity training is on the rise. Since the last couple of years, almost everyone who works in the business world or for the government gets exposed to this therapeutic method sooner or later.

Often this occurs in training programs that are not necessarily referred to as 'sensitivity training,' but that do, in fact, follow the same principles.

A lot has been written about this topic, of course, but usually in a far broader context. It is my hope that this small booklet will be of use to readers who have an interest in forming a grounded view on sensitivity training.

The publisher
Zelhem, the Netherlands, December 4, 2015

1

Faith and science

The changing position of theology

In the Middle Ages, theology was the *regina scientiarum*, the queen of sciences. Theological science held a sovereign position during this entire era, especially during the heyday of scholasticism. Later, under the influence of Renaissance and humanism, the queen of sciences was once and for all dethroned and philosophy stepped up to the position. Until then, philosophy had held a humble position as the *ancilla theologiae*, the maid servant of theology. In post-Cartesian times, the struggle for hegemony between the subsidiary sciences of philosophy would flare up again and again.

Gradually, philosophy developed into a service-oriented discipline and in the twentieth century it took on the role of an *ancilla scientiarum*, a maid servant of science. Theology, meanwhile, had been banished into isolation. A long struggle commenced, aimed at reaching a satisfactory answer to the question of whether theology can be called a science. It was accompanied by a disheartening battle between faith and natural science - a battle that was to reach many sad heights over time. Old perceptions of the world and creation were subjected to severe criticism by scientists.

True fruitfulness requires us to deal with tough questions

In the last few decades of our time, the front seems to have permanently shifted. The relationship between faith and science today has the full attention of theologians. And rightly so. If theology wishes to avoid being permanently locked up in a ghetto, it is vital that theologians thoroughly consider the very real problems posed by behavioral and other sciences. Limiting ourselves to biblical science would be disastrous. We must not allow fear of the psychologization or sociologization of theological science to drive theology away to some island far from civilization, where only exegesis and biblical theology are practiced. A confrontation with questions put by psychologists and other scientists is both inevitable and necessary.

It is important that we approach individual, social and political issues from Scripture. However, this does not mean that we must stick rigidly to biblicistic paths. On the contrary. These paths are always unpaved and muddy, and it is easy to get stuck on them. Before long, we may find ourselves unable to set the wheels of our vehicle in motion due to the roughness of the terrain, and our vehicle will be stuck in the mud up to its axles. Oddly enough, this state of being stuck provides a kind of firmness that many people desperately long for. It is not the steadfastness of God's Word, but of man's limited perception. If this is our approach, theological science will not be able to offer real guidelines for the church or the world. We can only be truly fruitful in the church and the world as we witness - Bible in hand, and in words and deeds - in the tradition of the centuries, to the God of Israel and Christ Jesus. The Holy Spirit will lead us into all truth concerning the perfect will of God.

The idea of this booklet

The idea of this booklet is not to tackle the deeper questions underlying the relationship between Christian faith and science. Rather, our purpose is to investigate the appropriate Christian attitude towards certain new social phenomena in our increasingly secularized society. In this booklet, I would like, specifically, to deal with the group dynamic processes that have gained popularity under the name of 'sensitivity training.'

Very generally speaking, sensitivity training is a method used in a group setting with the purpose of increasing sensitivity, i.e. the sensitivity of the participants, in order to thus enhance interpersonal relationships. Under the guidance of an expert, participants are invited to live out their feelings fully and without inhibition in order to become more sensitive to themselves and others. Group interaction is very important in this process, as it teaches people to respond more spontaneously. This psychological expansion enables participants to reach the intended self-realization and to communicate better in social life.

In many countries, sensitivity training is gaining ground in secondary and university education, in educational institutions for tutors and social workers, in social education centers for working youngsters, in education centers for nursing staff, in the business community, and, finally, also in churches. It is, quite clearly, not a phenomenon that is practiced only on the fringes of society.

In this booklet, I will first explore the cultural and social backgrounds of this phenomenon and present a historical-theoretical picture of sensitivity training. After that, I will discuss the course of the group process, its purpose, and its terms and conditions. Finally, I would like to look at possible objections, dangers and adverse effects of sensitivity training and find an answer to the question as to whether there is a biblical basis for this therapeutic method, while reflecting on my own position on this topic.

2

Cultural and social backgrounds

Human needs in a technocratic society

For a correct understanding of sensitivity training, it is very important to be aware of social and philosophical developments in today's world. In our modern technocratic society, people need to be trained in human relations. Confrontation in a group setting answers that need, offering exactly what many people are looking for in a professionalized welfare state in which everything seems to center on status and prestige. Perhaps the feeling of emptiness and the mood of uselessness can be taken away through sensitivity training? Perhaps the tensions and pressures of social and economic life can be mitigated through sensitivity training? Perhaps modern man can find a wholesome remedy for his loneliness and restlessness in sensitivity training? Perhaps sensitivity training will add new meaning to life in a culture that is rapidly becoming dehumanized, showing more and more signs of alienation and disintegration?

While some people radically break away from society to reshape their lives in the fellowship of a commune, most are unwilling to go that far. Interestingly, some of the enriching experiences available in communal life can be acquired in far less time in a development group. In a development or confrontation group, all aggressive, hostile feelings of discomfort can be expressed. The group leader stimulates participants to do so. There are no restrictions, no taboos. Nothing is unacceptable. There is complete freedom; the only strict condition is complete honesty and a willingness among participants to show their true selves. All falseness must be eliminated in the pursuit of friendship and intimacy. The purpose - apart from experiencing the release of one's own individual development - is to cultivate a sense of community and group awareness. This means values and goals change. In sensitivity training, the group's values prevail over personal values.

Clearly, this behavioral therapy thrives in places where 'the American way of life' is the standard. In places in which age-old cultural and - more specifically - religious traditions hold sway, sensitivity training would cause a revolution. But what is more to the point is that there is less need for there.

A manifestation of existential thinking

From a philosophical point of view, some have - correctly, I believe - interpreted sensitivity training as a manifestation of existential thinking. Reflections on the ideal personality differ not only from culture to culture, but even from generation to generation. In group work, the existentialist view of freedom and authenticity prevails.

The group process would be entirely different if another set of people were to participate. For example, if the participants chose to suppress feelings, stick to social conventions, be guided by fixed principles, and accept mechanisms of defense, the group process would not unfold as it intended in sensitivity training. In Chapter 8 of this booklet, we will get back to this in more detail as we discuss the objections and dangers surrounding sensitivity training.

What is clear so far is that from the viewpoint of cultural philosophy and socio-psychology, the rapid rise of the group confrontation movement is perfectly natural. In the next chapter, let's try and shed some light on the historical background of sensitivity training.

3

A historical-theoretical overview

Sociometry and psychodrama

A name that invariably pops up in conjunction with the earliest origins of the development of sensitivity training is that of J. L. Moreno. Moreno not only developed the method of sociometry, but also of psychodrama. He can rightfully be considered one of the first people to have engaged in group confrontation. In sociometry, members of a certain group are expected to answer questions about mutual sympathies and antipathies. The summarized results are called a sociogram. It provides information about the structure of a group or a community.

More important for sensitivity training is the development of the method of psychodrama, a precursor of group confrontation. Psychodrama offers an image of the behavioral patterns of a certain person in a certain situation. Like other forms of sensitivity training, this approach relies on verbal and nonverbal methods to develop and to establish emotional interaction between the individual and the group.

Many conflicts arise from the fact that people behave rigidly and get stuck in certain roles. Psychodrama seeks to provide insight into these habitual roles by encouraging participants to act out their behavior and by providing them with skills for taking on possible alternative roles. Psychodrama has five elements:

1. The stage, which forms a live environment.

2. The subject, i.e. the patient, or the protagonist, who must enact parts of his life.

3. The instructor, who is both therapist and psychoanalyst, and as such must provide stimulating hints.

4. The staff, i.e. the therapeutic helpers, who take up a position between the protagonist and the instructor; and ...

5. The members of the public, whose role is to help the patient and become patients themselves.

The use of role reversal techniques is vital to psychodrama. To augment their effect, one of the helpers in the psychodrama program is given a specific role, i.e. that of the 'double.' The double's task is to enable the participant to see himself through another person's eyes. This relationship between patient and double is the most important and far-reaching interactive element in psychodrama. The purpose in psychodrama is catharsis, the mental change that comes about through spontaneous improvization. Rigid patterns cause a person to get stuck in a certain role, but in psychodrama, the patient can spontaneously choose another role - all in the protected context of the psychodrama exercise, with sympathetic therapists and co-patients.

The main figures within the sensitivity training movement were all pupils or followers of Moreno. One of them was social psychologist Kurt Lewin (1890-1947). Initially, a professor in Berlin, Germany, he fled to the United States in 1933. In America, he taught in Bethel

(Maine), among other places. Among his students were Ronald Lippitt of the University of Michigan, and Leland Bradford, co-founder, along with Lewin, of the National Training Laboratories (NTL) for Group Development. Lewin himself became director. Another one of his students was Kenneth Benne, who was connected to the Center for Human Relations at Boston University.

The first training group

Kurt Lewin had the honor of organizing the first 'training group' (T-Group). This happened during a summer project on Human Relations in New Britain, Connecticut, in 1946. Only later, in the 1940s and 1950s, did the aforementioned NTL start using the name 'sensitivity training' for the 'training group.'

Lewin's efforts gave the first big boost to the development of group psychology. His particular focus was on human interaction. He observed that democratically formed working groups operated in a much more pleasant and efficient manner than groups structured according to an authoritarian model. Lewin's first experiences with the training group, which were to take on huge significance later, was quite coincidental. It occurred during a discussion of what had been done during a working group session in the summer project on human relations. In the next year, as well as after his death, more and more experiments were carried out. The aim was to investigate the group dynamic process.

These activities met with a lot of opposition in scientific circles. Experiments, remember, are only reliable if they are not bound to time or place; they must be reproducible. This means the historical dimension in Lewin's approach was lacking. Opposition among scientists focused mainly on this non-historical aspect, as well as on the decidedly non-authoritarian nature of working in groups.

Personal development, self-fulfillment and group confrontation

In the late 1950s and early 1960s, more and more distinction was made between the development of the organizational skills for trade and industry, on the one hand, and the sensitive experience as a means of developing one's personality, on the other hand. The Human Growth Centers were established to foster self-fulfillment. The Esalen Institute, especially, became very well known. It is difficult to distinguish between sensitivity training, group therapy, basic confrontation and group confrontation. In this booklet, I will use a mixture of terms for the same basic concept.

I would like to draw your attention specifically to the term 'group confrontation.' The American psychologist Carl Ransom Rogers (1902-1987) was the first to apply this name to sensitivity training. Rogers had very specific thoughts about psychotherapy. He is the one behind the nondirective approach (counseling), in which the client's autonomy is emphasized. The client's feelings are 'mirrored,' so that he is confronted with himself. The conversation partner is merely there to serve. These principles are also applied in confrontation groups. First the free manifestation of feelings and thoughts is stimulated, then participants are called to account for their emotions and underlying motives.

The fact that sensitivity training has become such a fast-growing psychological movement in today's culture can largely be attributed to Rogers. It is not entirely unjustified to speak of group therapy as a craze. Sensitivity training has at times been recommended as a cure for all diseases.

Some have observed the religious zeal with which new 'converts' - those recently exposed to the experience of group confrontation - try to persuade other people to engage in sensitivity training. Psychoanalyst Fritz Redl has compared this to the popular healings in Central Europe's spring water. Jokingly, he spoke about healing through immersion in 'Bad Bethel.'

It is quite imaginable that many moonlighters found an enormous field of activity in countries in which the new, still little-known phenomenon of sensitivity training first appeared. These nonprofessional trainers of basic confrontation groups have put sensitivity training in a particularly poor light. If we want to make fair judgment on this form of psychological therapy, we cannot take our evidence from the sessions of such groups.

4

The development of group processes

Group processes

In the next section, as we look at group dynamics processes, I will deal exclusively with training or laboratory groups. In the previous chapter, we have already hinted at psychodrama. Other well-known forms of group training sessions include the 'marathon method,' with sessions that last longer than usual, and the synanon method[2], a more aggressive, even offensive method used for participants who share the same symptoms (e.g., drug addiction). We will look at these two methods a little more closely in the next chapter.

Group processes for sensitivity training have their own unique characteristics. Normally, the trainer will specify the objectives of the meeting and then keep his options open. This will obviously cause some confusion, which has a purpose: the absence of structures is the primary principle in this laboratory situation, as a sense of complete freedom creates a vacuum, in which feelings of uselessness and boredom emerge among participants. The seemingly passive attitude of the trainer often fuels harsh criticism. In the absence of any form of continuity, furious

---

[2] 'Synanon' was a slip of the tongue for 'Santa Monica,' as pronounced by a, probably drunk, commune resident. It was later adopted by the rest of the movement. In the movement's early stages, Charles E. 'Chuck' Dederich founded a drug rehabilitation center in Santa Monica, California. - *Publisher.*

outbursts of anger can occur. Neither is the next phase, in which group members are encouraged by the trainer to investigate one another's attitudes and personalities, often embraced with gratitude. However, having overcome their initial resistance and diffidence, participants will usually begin to give themselves away on major issues - at first hesitantly, and then more and more confidently.

An atmosphere of mutual trust

As all of this can be very painful, it is imperative that the trainer first creates an atmosphere of mutual trust. Once this has been established, participants are invited to openly judge one another. Both positive and negative aspects are brought to light. All of the statements made by participants, as well as the suspected underlying motives, are carefully considered. In this context, the group process is supposed to start its healing work. People experienced in group therapy say that at this point group members exhibit a certain natural capacity to share one another's sorrows and pains. Those on the receiving end accept this care and work at bringing about changes in their own attitudes. Throughout the process, all façades are broken down. Social manners fall away. Masks are not accepted, as they are perceived as a hindrance to deeper, more fundamental contact. Everything serves the so-called 'intensification process,' which we will discuss in the next chapter.

5

The objective of sensitivity training

Total inner change

The 'intensification process' I mentioned in the previous chapter, also known as 'basic confrontation,' is the ruling principle in sensitivity training. Its goal is a change in attitude and behavior - a total, inner change of intentions.

During the intensification process, participants receive 'emotional feedback' through a group discussion of each member's behavior. Each participant is told how he or she is perceived by the other participants. Participants are thus supposed to gain a deeper knowledge of self. This self-knowledge enables them to change their behavior in the group. Participants become more sincere and spontaneous in their interaction with others, while also gaining more self-confidence. The absence of structures stimulates openness. The trainer's role is to encourage the expression of thoughts and feelings, and to facilitate the overall process.

A joint sense of security is vital to the process. In this atmosphere of complete trust, all masks can be dropped and all defense mechanisms stripped away. As façades melt away, each participant gets to know himself and becomes more conscious of himself, while also developing more understanding for others. The general sense of responsibility increases and this leads to deeper interpersonal relationships. Individual members become both more resilient and more aware of other members' sensitivities. This is what is meant with the process of intensification, or the basic confrontation: it leads to a more direct and deeper form of communication based on honest feelings.

Different purposes in different settings

As we have seen, sensitivity training is applied not only in educational establishments, but also in institutions for social learning. It is important to note that in these different settings, the technique can be used for different purposes. In business, the focus tends to be on developing group skills, organizational efficiency, more effective decision processes - in short, the optimization of business performance. This is quite different from those settings in which sensitivity training is used to provide participants with emotional experiences aimed at facilitating self-analysis, personal development and improved social communication.

Marathon training is used for the same purposes as the abovementioned group training. The only difference is that marathon training sessions last longer. The purpose is to intensify and accelerate the process of emotional self-revelation, but also to encourage authentic communication free of social fears and defense mechanisms. The synanon method is a more aggressive confrontation method; it is considered an effective means to bring about the 'healing' of a drug addict. In this approach, the expressions by participants of ridicule, sarcasm and provocative humiliation play an important role. This verbal abuse, or 'punishment,' is said to have a positive effect on the group member subjected to it. This positive effect is the main reason for the success of this aggressive form of therapy.

6

Conditions for group therapy

Assessing or participating in group therapy

A lot of activities presented under the name of 'sensitivity training' have very little to do with the original concept. If you're interested in assessing - or participating in - some form of group therapy and you don't want to be misled, you have to define some basic criteria.

As a potential participant, the first question you must ask yourself is why you want to participate in sensitivity training. What are your expectations? Do you want to overcome feelings of loneliness, or uselessness? Do you want to become more spontaneous in your social life? Does your trainer want to help you improve your performance at university, in education or in business?

Next, you need to find out what the objectives and criteria are of the group you are thinking of joining, as well as whether the group is coached in a responsible manner. Is the trainer sufficiently qualified and experienced?[3] What are his theoretical convictions?

Finally, the so-called 'screening' phase is also important. Screening is the process of selecting participants on the basis of certain predetermined conditions. For instance,

---

[3] According to dr. Everett L. Shostrom, former director of the American Psychological Association (APA), positive answers to these questions are no guarantee that the training is sensible for every participant. Every group training is a tricky business and advance screening is always necessary. See also pages 31-32, 43-44. - *Publisher.*

applicants may be accepted on the basis of their willingness and ability to be completely open, their personal strength or their self-esteem. All of these qualities can be investigated in the screening phase. The purpose is to facilitate the best possible group interaction. As a candidate, you should always check whether the training program includes an introductory interview as well as serious follow-up after the sessions.

I have tried, in this chapter, to give as objective a picture as I can of the development of the group process and its conditions. In the next chapter, I'd like to share some fundamental objections to sensitivity training and some of the dangers I observe in it.

7

Sensitivity training: an evaluation

A meaningful debate

Sensitivity training has often received bad treatment from critics. Their vicious attacks are understandable, as sensitivity training represents a psychological movement that has profoundly impacted modern culture. The response given to these critics, however, has also often been below par. For instance, it has been suggested that the opponents of sensitivity training are mostly fascists - an accusation we can only choose to ignore. It has also been said that any aversion to sensitivity training reflects the neurosis of the opponent. In my view, none of this is conducive to having a meaningful debate on the value of group therapy for our society.

The neutrality of the trainer

In order to pass a reasonable judgment on sensitivity training, there is one key aspect we must look at more closely: the trainer's position in group confrontation. Is he as neutral as we are generally told? His questions, his invitations to participants to express their thoughts and feelings and his decidedly non-authoritarian way of speaking remind us of Carl Rogers' nondirective, client-oriented therapy. It seems clear that the trainer leading the sessions, regardless of his approach, cannot have the same role as the other group members. Unfortunately, this is rarely stated explicitly. While most sensitivity trainers claim neutrality, it would be better if they were to be frank about their position in the group and to openly outline the standards they apply to the group process.

There is no doubt, after all, that there are specific standards. This is evident whenever a confrontation group includes members who have attended sensitivity training before. These 'alumni' tend to overbear the other group members. The moment this happens, conventional taboos in interpersonal relationships have apparently been replaced by a new - and quite oppressive - set of standards.

A 'kill or cure remedy'

We noted before how proponents of sensitivity training tend to present it as some sort of universal remedy for all ills. It is, however, advisable to bear in mind that numerous psychologists have said group therapy is a 'kill or cure remedy,' as it may well have an adverse effect on certain psychological functions. While public opinion suggests group confrontation has only favorable effects, we should remember that people with less pleasant experiences may not be very eager to shout their feelings from the rooftops - for fear of being labeled pessimists or freaks.

Monitoring results objectively

There are no objective standards for measuring the permanent effects of group therapy. Of course, it is easy to kid people into believing in its effectiveness. Why else would people spend large amounts of time and money on it? It must work. However, the intended purpose of a change in interpersonal relationships is often not accomplished. The improvements are often neither significant nor lasting. Surveys have shown that about half of the participants suffer a 'relapse' later. Besides that, the concept of sensitivity training is based on many assumptions.

Another point of criticism is that a group of volunteer participants is incomparable with those participants' normal social environment. In group training, conventional standards are disregarded and new rules introduced. It would be impossible to apply the rules and regulations of sensitivity training in society as we know it. There is little or no room for sensitivity there, after all. This is why, in my view, the results of sensitivity training in education and business are less than impressive.

Risks

Even if sensitivity training does not necessarily lead to lasting improvements, is there any harm in trying it out? In my opinion, such a view reflects an unfounded optimism. Many group leaders have only had limited education. During training sessions, they exert enormous pressure on participants to change their identity. This assault on personality can sometimes have a traumatizing effect. The stimulation of self-examination during sessions can leave participants with burdens and inner conflicts they are unable to process on their own afterwards. Following the group sessions, participants are often left unprotected and without follow-up. Once in a while, psychotic breakdowns are known to occur. There have been several cases in which participants later had to consult a psychotherapist in order to deal with a damaged or destroyed sense of self-respect. Sensitivity training does not just involve mental health risks for participants faced with incompetent leadership. Even a competent trainer may expose some participants to serious risks, particularly if there is inadequate screening prior to the formation of the group. In the seemingly confidential setting of a sensitivity training group, participants can be tempted to give away too much. The so-called emotional feedback they then receive - pitiless, aggressive and sometimes even sadistic in nature - can make matters much worse. Many people lack the capacity to process their experiences without ending up in deep emotional or spiritual confusion. This is why, I believe, sensitivity training can lead to serious psychological disruption.

A very striking illustration of permanent damage brought about by sensitivity training occurs when one partner of a couple participates. Marriages have been ruined by this. For this reason, couples nowadays are usually advised to participate together. Another risk, given the intimacy that develops between participants, is that participants get so involved with each other as to threaten healthy marriages.

A pseudo-religious tendency

It is quite reasonable to consider sensitivity training as a pseudo-religious tendency in modern society. The training sessions can be compared with a religious retreat. To a greater or lesser extent, sensitivity training is all about seeking security. Other aspects also remind us of religious phenomena. The group formation and the uniformity remind us of the Christian concept of community. The method of self-accusation and criticism of others, aimed at bringing about a change in attitude and conviction, can be compared with the confession of guilt, repentance and being born again.

A form of spiritual nudism

I strongly object to this pseudo-religious form of confession. I view it as no less than a manifestation of spiritual nudism. Feelings and emotions are brought into the open without inhibition, in order for participants to be liberated from certain complexes and inner tensions. Personal inabilities and shortcomings are confessed in public, after which the group provides absolution. The pressure on solidarity, meanwhile, means the lowest individual moral standards become the norm.

My objection to group confession as a form of spiritual nudism has a Christian basis. Within the framework of Christian ethics, it is absolutely improper. Also, this spiritual nudism is sometimes connected to physical nudism - in the form of the so-called 'naked marathon.' Nude training sessions are believed to help participants break down barriers more quickly: the group will integrate and become therapeutically operative in less time. Sometimes, mind-expanding techniques are also applied. Certain psychedelic effects are applied to cause participants to reach the 'peak experience' of self-transcendence. At best, we could appreciate all this as an anticipation of the eschaton, i.e., an over-spiritual, and thus Spiritless, carnal attempt to anticipate the last days.

Group morality

Essentially, an anti-Christian tendency underlies sensitivity training. A person's inmost life is bared ruthlessly in a way reminiscent of brainwashing. Then the participant's thoughts and feelings are restructured in a certain direction. A common group morality emerges that is often at odds with Christian morality. Social conventions, shame and sexual taboos are not tolerated, as they merely alienate people from one another. Patriotism and marital fidelity become symbols of narrow-mindedness. Sticking up for social structures and personality stability ranks as old-fashioned. Realistic defense mechanisms are considered neurotic manifestations. A reserved attitude is a disgrace, as it reveals an insincere, unreliable attitude. All in all, a new kind of intolerance takes over - an intolerance of anything but the most extreme openness and uninhibitedness! All barriers between people are broken down. An old slogan is revived: freedom, equality and fraternity. Sensitivity training is a technique for changing people's minds in order for them to willingly submit to liberalization, equalization and socialization, under the tyranny of which there is no room for Christian persuasions or morals.

My main objection

This brings me to my main objection to sensitivity training: it does not recognize the authority of the Bible. In fact, it dangerously undermines it, since the Christian norms derived from the Bible are not recognized.

It is evident that sensitivity training is wildly successful in our secularized society. Back in 1935, Johan Huizinga wrote the following prophetic words about the deterioration of morals in his brilliant study *In the shadow of tomorrow:* 'The unifying validity of the Christian system of moral laws has lost all meaning to many people.' To which he added: 'Will now every notion of obligation be completely lost in this withdrawal of the theoretical basis? Apparently not. Either through some form of inertia or because of its deep roots in mankind's inner life, the Christian morale, in the dethroned form in which society has always accepted it, will continue to control public and private standards of moral conduct [sic].'

The latter no longer applies today. The dangers observed by Huizinga have come about. Christian morals have been assaulted from three sides: (1) philosophic immoralism, (2) certain doctrines of a scientific nature, and (3) esthetic-sentimental doctrines. Philosophic immoralism only exists within a select circle, and its significance is indirect. Far more pervasive, says Huizinga, is the relativization of morality that is implicit in both the scientific system of historical materialism and in the psychological concepts derived from Freud. Huizinga very clearly recognized the anti-Christian nature of modern psychological movements. The resistance against religion within these movements is very powerful. In sensitivity training, this becomes evident in the fact that participants are expected to cast aside moral laws, morality and common decency as pointless taboos.

The portrayal of man in the ideology of sensitivity training also differs widely from that of Christian theology (of reformational[4] origin). In a discussion with Carl Rogers, Martin Buber said: 'By nature, man is good and evil.' The reformational theology[4] and confession teach us that man has a natural tendency to hate God and his neighbor. Only through the Holy Spirit and through conversion and new birth can man be reconciled with God and his fellow-man, a reconciliation accomplished by our Lord Jesus Christ.

---

[4] Of course, this also applies to the theology within orthodoxy, in the widest sense of the word. - *Publisher.*

8

Is there a biblical basis for sensitivity training?

The upside of sensitivity training

Sensitivity training certainly has its appeal. In our rigid technocratic and rationally structured western culture, it is evident that we fall short in good, personal interaction and that the prospects of self-realization are under pressure. In a society that is increasingly controlled by aggression, it is only logical for a training method to emerge that promotes instinctive contacts between people. Objections aside, we may therefore recognize with gratitude that there are many good things in sensitivity training. It encourages more meaningful contact between people and the development of a more balanced personality. It also seeks to remove tensions and irritations in communication and to create more harmony. All this may have our sincere appreciation. Especially in our western society, where at every level genuine interpersonal contact has become so scarce, and loneliness has become such a problem, the encouragement of forms of interaction that are more attuned to our innermost feelings has real value. Besides the will and the mind, human emotions also must be given their legitimate place.

The testimony of Scripture also compels us to firmly advocate more sincere and open interaction among people, for the sake of both the individual and society as a whole. While in our day the love of many waxes cold (Matthew 24:12), Paul exhorts us to be kindly affectionate towards one to another with brotherly love, loving one another without dissimulation (Romans 12:9-10). The sum total of the commandments is: '(...) Thou shalt love thy neighbor as thyself. Love worketh no ill to his neighbor: therefore love is the fulfilling of the law' (Romans 13:9-10).

If the second table of the law is not obeyed, we may as well ignore the first table. If there is no compassion or solidarity, it is because of a lack of true Christianity. Love waxes cold - the love for God, and thus also for our neighbor. The Church of Christ should have a wholesome effect on the community: see how they love one another! This love is unconditional and is characterized by a sympathetic attitude towards those with whom it interacts. This genuine sympathy is a rare commodity in our time, even among Christians. People say: Christians are really something else! They are - but usually not in the way that statement is meant. Love waxes cold and, sooner or later, we will have to pay for it.

The end versus the means

On the one hand, then, sensitivity training is an attractive phenomenon. But on the other hand, we must note that it is also typical of a secularized society. In many respects, its purposes are quite justifiable. But its starting-point is highly doubtful. The assumption that authority and moral values merely hinder human development and interpersonal contact leads to obvious difficulties. This starting-point also adversely influences the ultimate purpose. Where authority and ethos are eroded, the call for sincerity and openness - in itself a justified call - is deprived of its nobility, for the sake of personal development and interaction. This is the pivotal issue we must face in any fair evaluation of sensitivity training. The de-Christianization of society has left its all-dominating mark on sensitivity training. The end does not justify the means.

Is 'Biblical sensitivity training' a contradiction in terms?

We must ask ourselves whether sensitivity training, in the strictest sense of the word, can even exist if we require its alignment with God's unique norms. Isn't that our only alternative, after all?! This raises another unavoidable question: is 'Biblical sensitivity training' not a contradiction in terms?

If we introduce the demands God places on each and everyone one of us, we will no doubt be accused of being dogmatic. We must bear in mind, however, that a neutral stand is impossible. Fortunately, this fact has gained more and more recognition in our days. We might suggest our accusers are like the pot calling the kettle black, as sensitivity trainers removes one set of norms merely to set up a new ideology in its place. They seek to introduce a different society - a society with another morality, i.e. one that follows a Marxist pattern.

The heart of the problem

But theology and ideology are not equal alternatives. In its deepest sense, ideology is idol-logy. Ideals become idols. We must choose God or the idea. God or the idol. And the two are not equal. This brings us to the very heart of the problem of sensitivity training. Our objection to sensitivity training is not that its humanistic worldview stresses individual development, but that it promotes breaking down taboos, exercising violence against the conscience, and undermining the notion of God. Sure, it focuses on the wellbeing of man in his personal development and in his interaction with others, but God, in Christ, should be central in all of this. Only then can God receive due honor. If we seek humaneness, we must first seek Christ.

True renewal is contingent on conversion

So how should we respond to sensitivity training and the underlying need it seeks to meet, both from an individual point of view and from a political, social and ecclesiastic viewpoint? To begin with, we should never accept forced participation in sensitivity training sessions, certainly if the objectives and principles are not explicitly stated. Obviously, noncommittal participation is not an option. In the group process, one cannot take on the attitude of a spectator. It would not be a very constructive approach anyway. Instead, we face the task of making a sensible contribution to constitutional decision-making on this matter.

From a political point of view, parliamentary democracy obliges us to guard the freedom of education and development. From a biblical point of view, we are called to testify in word and deed that true freedom is found only in the subjection of nation and government to God's law as it has been given to us within the framework of the promises of the Word. True social and educational renewal are contingent on conversion to God. Psychology and sociology lead us to believe a change in social structures and mentality will do the job. But the Bible tells us we must turn to God. This latter must come first; then the former will follow. We must not despise science, but neither must we overestimate it.

The whole field of behavioral sciences is deeply secularized and therefore poses serious questions. Not that we are to reject scientific methods as such, but indiscriminately employing certain sensitivity training techniques may cause us great harm. We must be alert. Those with relevant expertise have a particular responsibility. I believe they have crucial battles to fight on this front and that it is a miracle if their faith comes through these battles unscathed.

The Bible and the Church

We must draw our views on political and social questions as well as on educational problems, from the Bible. There is no antithesis between modern culture and Christianity. The Bible has power of expression in all fields of life. If and when we fail to confess that, we ourselves contribute to the secularization of our society.

But that is not all. This is not merely about us influencing decisions made by Christian organizations and political parties. That is important, of course, but it is not the only thing that counts; pretending it is, is just one more way of contributing to the de-Christianization of society - regardless of our intentions. Ultimately, all our activities should be directed at the Christianization of public life and culture. Each of us must do what his hand finds to do. And we must join forces, working together side by side. Our fellowship is more than the sum of its individual members. In addition to our combined actions in the social field, I would like, last but not least, to mention the role of the Church of Christ, the fellowship of the saints. The church does not exist for herself; rather she has a significant task with respect to public life. Her prophetic and confessional calling is meant to contribute to the true wellbeing of society. And in this situation of ours, special attention may be given to the self-realization of man and improved interpersonal communication.

9

Conclusion

In closing, I would like to share some comments made by dr. Everett L. Shostrom (1921-1992) and prof. dr. Manfred Lütz. The late dr. Shostrom was a psychotherapist, author and president of the American Psychological Association (Humanistic Psychology) from 1973 to 1974. Prof. dr. Manfred Lütz is a professor of psychiatry and psychotherapy, director of a psychiatric hospital in Cologne, Germany, and a theologian.

In *Interpersonal Growth and Self Actualization in Groups* (1973, MSS Information Corporation, New York), edited by Raymond M. Maslowski and Lewis B. Morgan, the following quotes[5] by dr. Shostrom appeared; they were taken from an article in *Psychology Today* (1969, volume 2, no. 12, pages 37-40):

'Never participate in a group encounter with close associates, persons with whom you have professional or competitive social relations. Be worldly wise, or healthily paranoid, about this. As a corollary, never join a group that fails to make clear and insistent distinctions between the special environment of the group and the equally special environment of society. You should be told crisply, that everything occurring within the group must be considered vitally privileged communication. You should always feel that the warm, vigorous disalienation that flowers in a good group is to a certain extent designed to suggest the

---

[5] Quotations from the section 'Critical Issues' on pages 82-86 in the chapter 'Group Therapy - Let the Buyer Beware.'

richness of possibilities - in terms of self-knowing and other-knowing - and does not by any means imply a rigid code of behavior. In these matters, consult your common sense - it probably is one of the worst enemies you have, but it still is an entirely internalized enemy, hence deserving of notice.

Never join an encounter group on impulse - as a fling, binge or surrender to the unplanned. Any important crisis in your life has been a long time in preparation and deserves reflection. The intense, sometimes apocalyptic experience of the group can be most unsettling. A trained person responsible for a meaningful session would not throw precariously balanced persons into a good encounter group.

Also consider that any reputable professional (a qualified psychologist or psychiatrist) has a vital stake in any group he runs, or in any group whose leader he has trained and continues to advise and coach. This means there must always be a *formal*, and not an *informal*, bond between the trainer and the psychologist or psychiatrist.'

Another important thing to remember is that the role of modern psychology and psychotherapy in society has - and must have - its limitations, as these sciences 'cannot say anything about existential things, such as the existence of God'[6], in the words of Manfred Lütz, the German

---

[6] Manfred Lütz, *Gott: Eine kleine Geschichte des Größten* (Pattloch Verlag, Munich, 2007), page 24. Lütz devotes an entire chapter to the philosopher Ludwig Feuerbach and his statement that God is a projection of man. This booklet is not the right place to discuss this in detail. I advise you to read Lütz's book if you want to know more about it. Perhaps it is sufficient to mention the response made by John Lennox, the Oxford math professor and philosopher of science. In an interview in *The Times*, he was asked to comment on Stephen Hawking's statement that 'Religion is a fairy story invented for people

theologian and professor of psychiatry and psychotherapy. 'Tensions arise when the existential frameworks, morals and worldviews of the trainer suffuse the training sessions, which they invariably do - usually without taking into account the morals and views of other participants.'

Lütz also says that 'It is understandable from a psychological point of view that people wish to eliminate God - as far as He exists. It is argued that God should be relegated to the realm of private life. We will say more later - this is in Lütz's book of course - about such 'emasculated' conceptions of God for the bourgeois living-room, but let me say here and now that a God with only a role in our private lives, is no God at all, but rather a living doll, a sissy, an object of ridicule.'[7]

If we want to evaluate sensitivity training on the basis of a single Bible verse, we may well end up with Galatians 2:20. Sensitivity training says, 'Not I, but the group.' The Christian, however, confesses, 'Not I, but Christ.'

---

who are afraid of the Dark.' Lennox responded: 'To this I can only say that atheism is a fairy tale for people afraid of the Light!'
[7] Lütz, pages 31-32.

www.ingramcontent.com/pod-product-compliance
Lightning Source LLC
Chambersburg PA
CBHW061721120626
46550CB00003B/1314